THIS BOOK BELONGS TO

....

5/16" Staff Width,
10 Staves per Page

PLEASE LEAVE A REVIEW BECAUSE
WE WOULD LIKE TO HERE YOUR FEEDBACKS
AND SUGGESTIONS TO MAKE BETTER
PRODUCTS AND SERVICES FOR YOU.

YOU ARE REALLY APPRECIATED!

HOPE YOU LIKE IT.

GET MORE BOOKS,
SCAN HERE!

Made in the USA
Monee, IL
10 December 2022

20667475R00057